INDIA POEMS

HELEN FOGARTY

ISBN: 978-0-936319-05-6
1.Poetry   2.Oneness University   3.Golden City, India

Singing Stars Press
Milton, New York

a hug from the Source of All
Auroville bus list
blessings of India
connections
Golden City: walking home
her smile could heal the world
Holy Mother's words to me
glimpses
in India's womb
in the arms of beauty
Indian insects
Indian plumbing
is this your country?
my first lizard
my second lizard
slowly inside
snapshots
the old dog
the world reaches out its hundred million arms
third lizard
this is what nourishes us each morning
this morning's lesson
visiting the Golden Temple
weed pickers
welcome to Indian night
what the laundry woman found

These words poured through me
when I spent a month in
southern India at
Oneness University
nearly a decade ago.
I recently reread them in
my journal and I want to share
what it was like for me to be
in Golden City, listening,
learning, and feeling.
Whether or not you know India,
I hope that you enjoy the poems
that came from Her,
the Great Mother.

a hug from the Source of All

here is the face of the immense Mother
Her radiant heart of joy
here is She – plugged into divinity
full up with the force that made the world

here She is in human form, blessing Her children
and this fair Earth, giving because She cannot help
but do so   She cannot be other than She is

the stone in my heart has rolled away
the bone gates of my chest are opening
my jawbone loosens and shuddering's in my head
the taste of the rose fills this air.

Auroville bus list

faith and flowers
room-sized banyan tree – many feet firmly rooted
yards from its mother trunk
a fern 7 feet tall
the Mother's red rock earth feeding everything
this place of filth and fecundity
stenchy toilets unflushable and fetid
black marble sinks fit for a palace but waterless
deepdug gashes in Mother Earth's red skin,
water resting just 2 feet beneath
tall trees which, back in New York, grow short
here with white long-necked flowers fragrant in wet air

the people, the people, the people working on everything
day and night, lying on a stoop under a shawl, picking weeds
from grass and piling them across a useless lawn,
thin dark workers, women and men, our family,
speaking a language we do not know, carrying bundles of:
green leaves, food, cloth, plastic buckets, bananas,
hardship and poverty, they're washing and selling,
biking and peeing on walls, pedaling carts and cooking,
packing and sewing, standing and looking, smiling
and scowling, talking and playing board games
on a sidewalk corner until the next fare comes
sweet-voiced music and swaying tunes cascade
like gemstones in this braising, welcoming air.

blessings of India

a remarkable erratic watch which stops
when it's tired, and works beautifully
when it desires a long, puzzling stretch
of reliability

tiny, humless mosquitoes, stealthily
administering 2 bites per evening
until I solve the complex mystery
of the fan overbed   now they have
moved on to some fanless dreamer
whose quiet air's no threat of dessication

the "ok tested" sticker on the broken toilet paper holder;
"ess ess" brand water faucets ("eat eat?" perhaps this logo
to remind us of the connection between eating
and why we are in this room now)

tiny ants everywhere (me included), even tinier ones
drowned in a tight-lidded jar of coconut oil
their tiny tiny stings drowned also
who, I ask you, would take coconut oil to India?
does such a one deserve to collect moribund ants?
no, but here they are, drowned in grease

and since I have no "self " who exactly is eating
this earthly food from "tall boy" cutlery?
am I tall boy or was I in an earlier life?
If I am anyone at all, it's "tall girl," perhaps.

connections

in this place of great peace
is a place of disturbance
where earth is churned and opened
and there live the weeds: a few
I almost recognize – South Indian versions
of some green friends from home
a vetch creeps along, its flowers slightly skewed
from what I've known, but it's completely vetchy

seed tops of grass, a blueprint for our dorm's
3-pronged ceiling fans, stand, as does
our northern grass, in the "off" position

a would-be sunflower, perhaps, sprawls
among green tangles, in gorgeous contrast
to the rust-red tiles being neatly laid along
the walkers' long, linear path

some small flowers, faces opened to the sun,
call out, and possibly a type of milkweed,
but this I do not know   like someone
I met before I was born, you look vaguely familiar

overnight a dark oval-leaved vine has crept another foot
along the walkway, like an impetuous aunt, and more
small flowers bloomed above rosettes of leaves

small Norfolk Island pines are planted
by the meditation hall in this far place
them at least I recognize, and wonder
what they think of India

the plant resembling milkweed has flowered
to a tropical version of morning glory: big
white   luscious   what artist made you?

I wish I could name you, floral sisters,
for all the Mother's girls are cousins,
however many times removed,
and these are the weeds, remember?

low beds of flowers – rose, yello, white,
have just been planted, but I prefer the wild –
their unknowable patterns –
they which grow where *they* choose
among long metal pipes and lumps of this and that
you are where you belong
unwatered and untended, you thrive
at least one of so many who pass each day
appreciates your perfectly considered lives.

glimpses

I'm out of bed and in the bathroom
the sink's filled with tiny specks of black —
suicided insects and one single mosquito
intent on a final sip of my delicious Hawaiian punch
here's an unswattable pest: a thorough professional
it gets its drink   I brush my teeth
we are restored to day.

this morning after breakfast 2 male dogs
had an altercation at a sand pile
it attracted a small crowd, human and canine,
of interested bystanders
come to experience the growling, posturing pair

returning the same path later in the morning
there was the victor of sorts, little more
than a sack of bones, lying at the edge of sand,
a king in his castle, alpha and asleep.

my perceptions re last night's laughfest:
it felt ok, but crazy maniacal laughs are not my speed:
they were too weird, too loud, too much, too soon,
and I felt pity for one young man, a very skinny,
cosmic being who's not spoken in over 2 years,
who laughed with such intensity
I couldn't fathom anyone laughing so strongly
for so long, and who fell to his knees while walking
the aisle to the front of the room, and rose

with help from his fellows   they said he rarely
stops to eat, but after half an hour of giggling, eastern
ripples of merriment pouring over us from the bunch
before us, the young man eventually left us, laughing
while we tried to understand what we just could not.

Golden City: walking home

a roof light holds a galaxy
of swirling stars with wings
that celebrate the night self

big blanket of heat encompasses us all
in calm, patient always

who questions this peace?
even the dogs are dimmed,
their watchful eyes on hold

earth's fever drops, her sun at rest,
and evening sighs a slow mantra

how can we not be fortified
in the rhythm of the Mother,
vaster and more nurturing than breath?

her smile could heal the world

and every creature in it
a smile of eyes, lips, being
that pours its light
into everyone receiving

noiseless, a smile is powerful
carrying all you need to know
pure feeling flows like honey
expanding to the form of formlessness

what a gift, this smile —
free, gentle, shining.

Holy Mother's words to me

as we sat   we meditated
upon the golden lotus at the crown
a throne for Mother inside the chakra
I spoke to Her and understood the birds,
those birds I've seen as messengers,
were from Her   so I asked how I would know
Her presence in other ways and She said in music,
in beautiful light, especially lavender dusk,
in beauty in general   She is there

She's been sending me signs for a long time
and I've seen them, appreciated them, but not
recognized them as Hers before this knowledge:
what a gift She's given and I've received it.

In India's womb

I am missing my mother, my Mommy,
she who left me 54 years
since, sickening unto death
and walking, somehow, away from me

here, I am meeting another Mother
where She abides, alive in Her power
and compassion for us all, even me.
unaccompanied one, broken-hearted girl

India has heard my tears, more drenching
than before: I used to think I knew myself
as the one with nothing, but no, for I
have made acquaintance with the rest of me
she who lives beneath the hard skins of grief and rage

in this hot wet season a shedding has begun
can I allow myself to experience how it feels to feel
whatever it is that I've feared always,
without commentary, nor distraction nor pretence nor anything?

I pray I may learn how, as I thought I knew,
that the only way out is through,
and with the help of Grace, I will come to the doors
and open them and, finally, go through.

in the arms of beauty

she is one of 5, sitting in a line of sheeted chairs in front of us
all in the meditation hall   her head is shaved and she is tall
this I see, from the rear of this huge space, encumbered with
my limited self, and from these 5 pours the bright face of God

they are all so young and full of bliss,
mirroring our best dreams of what is love:
16 awakened beings here are living in the light
I feel the spaciousness inside, when with
their slow procession down the middle path,
they've taken seats and there they sit communing:
a wave of peacefulness flows in, our chance to be
inside the space of total love   I wait to move
to this enlightened one whose arms will finally enfold

my heart, despite the tranquil place, is pounding
as I drop to my knees, the perfect place to be,
within this being's field a kind of intense yielding
I lift my eyes to her breath-taking face, her beauty beyond human
as she accepts me in, into her arms, to her caressing heart,
where I expand like an opening bloom
where all I've ever required is more than ever here
I'm filling up with love, but cannot say its names

only, only this – when close enough to be inside
and full of all I need to live   so brimming that tears fall
I cannot understand how this immense embrace can come to me
again and again I fall into its depths,
feeling its energy in every particle of me

here I could live until the end of bodily life,
dissolving in the sweet arms of God:
I'm welcomed to the realms of gold.

Indian insects

they crawl (centipedes on the walkway)
they march (tiny pale ants who live behind
a bathroom faucet or behind the outlet near my bed)

black bugs recline in the sink at night
too stunned by the experience of white
to continue to live through morning

some emerge from unlikely places, from behind
snack bars boxed in the bedside table,
from my carry-on bag unzipped beneath the bed

an occasional moth perches near light
practicing mothness   even the flies, hanging
in webs, await the spider's dance, unstruggling

have they all learned the lessons of this place?
are they paying attention to experience
with pure acceptance of all events befalling?

all except the mosquitoes, a-borning,
they do not plan to die
and accepting fate is not their thing.

Indian plumbing

too stiff   too old   spotted and crochetty
adorned with fabulous monikers "ess ess"

the hotel sink with reluctant start and
impetuous cascade that soaks my sleeve

hot water heaters that drip when off, but keep
their warmed water somewhere away from me

gurgles   moans   and many protestations:
leave me be, for I am old and need my rest

unflushing toilets: I have already given too much!
or torrential waterfalls that wash our sins away

onto those tropical fruits I long to eat but dare not:
pineapple   sapote   melon   lime   mango

Is this your country?

I unzip my bag and a mosquito flies out
such mosquitoes so small and swift
I cannot manage to swat one, even
after it has sipped my blood

here all the dogs are from the same family –
spotted, tan, bone-bare or only slightly emaciated,
their eyes are Asian and they know something –
likely something more than I do,
surely they know something about difficulty,
about sleeping on asphalt and the occasional
negative interaction with kin

the workers do their jobs well:
they feed us, and clean for us,
sweeping, wiping, removing our refuse
like a bunch of competent mothers.

my first lizard

you're perhaps 3" of almond-colored self
holding the vertical, on a bathroom tile

with that soft body and black, punctuated eyes,
you look benign to me, almost a dasa, tan and alert

but who knows, perhaps you're a venomous boy,
that translucency, however, persuades me otherwise

are you in camouflage? do you hide in barley gruel
or in the "broken-wheat" upma which gassed me up
so perfectly one recent breakfast?

whatever you prefer, even insect-hunting in the night
bathroom, my thanks for making your appearance

a small being of the evening
practicing the miracle of life.

my second lizard

same bathroom   different stall
this one so fast its darkness startled me

please, o lizardy one, please eat all the mosquitoes,
the ones that do not buzz but bite our ankles
in the dim night and fly over the shower walls
into your stall when you turn on the light to bathe

I hope this darker lizard's hue means her diet
was full of mosquito selves crunching like chips
in her mysterious jaws.

slowly inside

beginning with the feet, I'm
searching for balance on the hard floor
that rings the meditation and the dining halls

slowing my pace is challenging
something in me wants to race, but no:
I try the turtle's way
though focus is often outside myself,
and it takes a village to gaze me in

that afternoon, walking past the papaya peelers,
through stripes of pillars shadowing sun,
comes a dragonfly
it boards my left shoulder and stays with me
a long minute or two   I am honored
her dragonfly steps feel stately and slow

my child's mind created fear of these flying pointers:
imagining the mother of all stings, I jumped
when darning needles arrived in August,
and did not want to know them
but this sweet lady alighted on a part, a part of me
that sometimes causes pain, and left, perhaps,
her healing footprints behind.

snapshots

a bright green parrot perched one morning
on the metal bones of a being-built building

thin dark workers, women and men, our family,
speaking a language we long to know

night-hidden monkeys chattering
amongst themselves for just one evening

a few souls silently sitting near me
in the lobby as day again is born.

the old dog

has been learning to eat again
everything in him has shrunk except the soul
living in his eyes   his coat is shabby
and marked: the story of him

once, perhaps, he lived his life with joy,
once trotted and ran – defended his turf,
choose his wives and fathered pups

now he is stillness, holding a kind of watching,
a kind of deep pain no creature should have to carry,
a well of suffering and endurance

a wish for some remaining peace
and death without lingering –
the very last kindlings of hope.

the world reaches out its hundred million arms

the grasshopper who climbs onto my foot as I wait
with all the others outside the huge temple

one half moon splits into
tangerine slices in a dish of water

a dragonfly: catching a ride on my shoulder
as I walk behind the dining hall

the woman whose maniacal laughter pushes
almost every one of my "should" buttons

small white moths bathing
in bathroom light

a gift at the dining hall trash bin
from a woman who tells me her journey

the dasas (young teachers), grounded and clear,
who look into your eyes and see

16 celestial objects (1 for each of the awakened beings here)
which appear miraculous in photographs of last night's sky

third lizard

you came to me by rumor   I have not seen you yet
the woman 2 beds down saw you last night on her windowsill
just before sleep   according to her you are "this big" and
fat from eating a big bunch (cluster, horde, flock?) of bugs,
I hope   are you big enough to contain perhaps a hundred
of those tiny bathroom lizards?   that's a large lizard to me

what else do lizards eat?   I stash my vulnerable bags
of cashews and goji berries and insert them into the vault
of a zippered bag behind my bed   I do not imagine that I
could handle a night raid on my snacks   and do forgive me,
lizards, if I malign you with my worries   for me an invisible
reptile in a room where I sleep is an incompletely imagined
entity   please introduce yourself tomorrow, preferably
with menu of your favorite foods in claw; and I will see
what I can do   and please, do not scurry uninvited into
any of my dreams   your indulgence is much appreciated

ps: today the only other woman who saw you told me you
were only "this big" – a chameleon-sized sister of the 2
I fast glimpsed on the toilet's walls before
they scurried into their reptilian business.

this is what nourishes us each morning

water fills my mouth when I eat you – sun-filled papaya:
thus starts breakfast these sauna mornings

sometimes it's salty cornflakes with warm buffalo milk,
sometimes it's an Indian ferment: iddlis or uttapam

always yogurt, thin and bumpy, but good, good, good,
especially with banana sliced into a copper bowl

dessert's a metal glass of smoky ginger tea mixed with
equal milk, a delicate treat for the delicate gut.

this morning's lesson

I feed you so that I too shall be fed
I straighten up so that you will notice this work
when it is time to clean I take good care
of you, hoping you will reciprocate

much that I do for you reflects my needs
but you are not a child who needs a teacher
and where do you keep the mirror
into which you gaze?

visiting the Golden Temple

we come, just before dusk
and here night falls from a great height –
a great stone descending fast

we group in the center of one immense unfinished hall
and start to chant the Moola mantra which rises into
far off marble vaults like a horde of angels winging away

afterward, my fingers curve – a living glove –
around glowing pink marble globes topping hundreds
of balcony poles upright in darkening air.

weed-pickers

3 women in saris full of colors sit,
knees angled, on this green green grass

they work, like all I see here, slowly, on the lawn
as piles of weeds grow into small heaps before them

though they have little, peace surrounds
while they talk to each other in their true voices.

welcome to Indian night

where I waken from a dream like a movie I would never go to see,
a dream of secrets and important world-bound information
I acquire that changes my life into one of ducking into
fancy restaurants to avoid government agents,
spotting the feeding Queen through an upstairs window
I've written a story that all must read and somehow
Mary, another writer I know from yoga class, is here
she's a high level official who helps this information
enter the world   I have written this missive
based on something I somehow know   if only Mary hadn't
managed to cut up a section of the hardwood floor in my house
now it's covered with sawdust and scratches, but I'm not
convinced it's ruined, maybe it just needs cleaning

while this intrigue's on: there are messages in the freezer
(I think) and cars driving me to some unknown destinations
very very fast   I have become part of something
that has such major consequences that I myself
am in the dark about what impact will come.

what the laundry woman found

tweezers, candy and snack wrappers, lint,
paper products (pristine and questionable),
dead ants, lot of hair paraphernalia: clips,
headbands, combs and such, pens, lists,
buttons and bows, crumpled tissues, and
many, very many, oceans really, of tears.

www.ingramcontent.com/pod-product-compliance
Lightning Source LLC
Chambersburg PA
CBHW021149020426
42331CB00005B/973